PRIZEWINNING POEMS and NEW COLLECTIONS

Gwendolyn Carr

OLD AND NEW
"Prizewinning Poems and New Collections"

© Gwendolyn Carr

© 2015 Chemical Publishing Co., Inc. All rights reserved.

No part of this publication may be reproduced, stored in a retrieval system or transmitted in any form or by any means, electronic, mechanical, photocopying, recording, scanning or otherwise, except as permitted under Sections 107 or 108 of the 1976 United Stated Copyright Act, without either the prior written permission of the Publisher. Requests to the Publisher for permission should be addressed to the Publisher, Chemical Publishing Company, through email at info@chemical-publishing.com.

The publisher and the author make no representations or warranties with respect to the accuracy or completeness of the contents of this work and specifically disclaim all warranties, including without limitation warranties of fitness for a particular purpose.

ISBN: 978-0-8206-0398-8

www.chemical-publishing.com
Printed in the United States of America

Previously Published in:

A Far Off Place Anthology
A Lenten Day Book
American Poetry Annual
American Poetry Anthology
An Advent Daybook
Byline
Christian
Christianity Today
Contemporary Poets of America and Britain–Anthology
Dan River Anthology
Diamonds In A Daisy Field
Episcopal Voice
Eternity
European Seminar Itinerary, Gordon College
Great Poets of Our Time
Green County Council On The Arts
Honey For A Woman's Heart
Hope Whispers–Anthology
Idiom
International Library of Poetry
International Women's Day
Legacy of Words
Lenten Journey
Mars Hill Review

Massachusetts Poetry Society—Anthology
Midstream
Midwest Poetry Review
New Oxford Review
New Voices Anthology
North Central Review
Poetica
Sandcutters
Stars and Songs
Stillpoint
Take A Break
The Anthology of New England Writers
The Gordon
The Lyric
The Parish Voice
The Pegasus Review
Voices For Peace
Waterways
Z Miscellaneous

"for my dear grandson, Benjamin, in gratitude".

About the Author:

Boston born Gwendolyn Carr has published three books of poetry: Stars and Songs, Diamonds In A Daisy Field, and Legacy of Words. With her husband, G. Lloyd Carr, she co-authored Fierce Goodbye on the topic of suicide. Seventeen of her poems are included in that volume. Her poems have been set to music and performed at various venues. The annual Gordon College Christmas Gala included her poetry on numerous occasions. Her poems have also appeared on specialty–designed greeting cards.

She is a professional dressmaker/designer who has worked with fabrics since childhood. She and her husband make their home on Boston's North Shore, very near the ocean.

Table of Contents

PRIZEWINNING POEMS

A Poem Speaks	1
Against Fixity	3
Alienation	5
Am I Listening?	7
Artist's Dream Life	9
As The World Turns	11
At This Time	13
Awakening	15
Betrayal	17
Chartres Votives	19
Daisies Tell	21
Desire	23
Dream Sequence II	25
Express Train	27
Georgia O'keeffe	29
Gloucester	31
Legacy II	33

Manhattan Cityscape	35
Military Cemetery	37
Music	39
Royalty II	41
She Knows Her Strength	43
Sunrise Come	45
The Invitation	47
To Fall In Love	51
Tongues Of Spirit	53
Unexpected	55
Unnumbered	57
When Gabriel Came	59
Within Her	61
Wives	63
Your Garden	65

NEW POEMS

African Wife	67
Angel Watch	69
At The Party	71
Autumn	73
Awake	75
Beauty	77
Before	79
Beyond Reason	81

Books Equal Friends	83
Butterflies–After Robert Frost	87
Geraniums	89
Heron	91
January Thoughts	93

POEMS OF EXILE

Adam And Eve	95
Consequence	97
Adversary	99
Woman	101
Choice	103
Eden	105
In The Beginning	107
Inheritance	109
Oh Adam, What Have You Done?	111
One Couple, Two Leaves	113
Outside	115
Source	117
The Evil One	119
The Two Of Us	121
After Words	123
Twentieth Century Adam And Eve	125
After Adam	127

Author's Forward:

This book begins with prizewinning poems from 1982 to 2015. A few new poems make up the middle, and the last section entitled, *Poems of Exile* is the result of my long fascination with "the beginning" as recorded in scripture. I have attempted to present the story of creation in various ways, from various viewpoints. The characters are the same: God, Adam, Eve, Satan, and us.

Gwendolyn Carr

PRIZEWINNING POEMS

A POEM SPEAKS

Before you, I was; and wait
to rise from limbo to a cause,
from the depths of your being
to fulfillment of mine.

I know the long struggle,
the dry time, the pause,
before graven images
clamor for applause.

But hold this before you
bold sculptor of the line:
All your brilliant images
are already mine.

AGAINST FIXITY

Eons pass–I watch
the river in its mad descent,
the lashing winds that strip the crops,
the radiant rose of yesterday
fade and wither 'til it drops.

One season shoves the last one out
as if to say, enough of you.
As robins hurry to the south,
winter's glaze comes in on cue.

The silent motion of all things
however infinitesimal,
conspires against stagnation:
The constant change and flux,
the quickly fading rainbow,
the sages turning into dust.

ALIENATION

So long away,
you've now
become a stranger,
someone knocking
at my door
in winter's cold.
And I am locked
inside, in rooms
where fairy tales
are told,
and will not answer
'til the spring,
when all the world
is wakening.
And could it be
my open door
will draw you in,
my gypsy kin,
from all your years
of wandering?

AM I LISTENING?

I haven't stopped,
–not yet.
Slowing down
is not the same.
The noisy world
still calls,
insists I do it now.
One more fragment
of the day spent down–
one more detail done.

But angels wait
to hear the sigh,
the giving in
to solitude
where I at last
can hear the Voice
that, in the stillness,
speaks.

ARTIST'S DREAM LIFE

Asleep, I live another life
where famous people come and go.

Consider Michelangelo.
His fingers sketching
on the wall
where petals fall
from Georgia's stems,
and Nureyev
leaps through them.
Mahler strikes a somber note,
awakens Bach
who grabs his coat,
exiting before the rhyme
Emily executes on time.
Then Domingo flings his voice,
and all the angels join. Rejoice!

Another life, another song,
another dance
when things go wrong,
a simple word from sage's mouth,
a bright new painting
strung about,
all with angel's special blessing,
keeps me dreaming—never dressing.

AS THE WORLD TURNS

Leave the noise,
for night is now upon us
as silently we sleep
we dream
and do not know ourselves.

We cannot hear
a falling tear,
or footsteps of a centipede.
The sailing of a westward cloud,
the slowly rising purple mist
or hanging of a blazing star
are hushed,
as if a tryst in heaven
made them what they are.

All are moving without sound
or punctuation in the land.
No rude report or cymbal's clang
but quiet as the evening sand,
and as the winter air is clear,
it is in silence that we hear.

AT THIS TIME

No argument with Caesar,
The line of David must be traced,
and taxes paid,
no matter how the stars are placed,
or where a baby might be laid,
or if a mother found it hard
to navigate the way.
Caesar's word must be obeyed!

No argument with angels.
Their vibrant song will still be heard,
reverberate,
though other songs have since appeared
and had their day, but can't compare,
while heaven's notes and heaven's news
still echo in the field.

AWAKENING

Months have passed
while tulips slept alone,
unseen.
Now, winter takes its cover off
revealing tender shoots
of green.

And touching one delicious
bud,
I cannot help but wonder
how it managed
resurrection
after winter's cruel plunder.

BETRAYAL

She fled
her father's house,
putting the miles between them,
strung the anger
like a cord
around her recent freedom
–much wiser to live far–
alone.

And did I fail to mention
his raw, misplaced attention?

CHARTRES VOTIVES

Three banks of them
flicker in the gloom,
raise the light
in the vaulted room,
absorb the prayers
whispered for the dead,
while I look on
gazing instead
at the shadows cast
on the great stone wall.

As I recall,
mother's been gone
for thirty years.
I blink through tears,
and pray she knows
the candle I light
for all it glows
cannot outshine her vivid life.

DAISIES TELL

Daisy flowers regard the tongue
as awkward, unreliable,
when young men yearn
to speak of love.
They offer petalled substitutes,
a death of simple parts,
scattered to the wind
for the joining of true hearts.

So let the petals speak
their litany of love;
in one untimely sacrifice
declare the bond
that young men hardly speak of.

DESIRE

A hunger in the heart for love
will always be acute.
And when the mating game is on
Cupid flies, ready to shoot
the stumbling pair, who,
looking here, searching there,
meet by chance, or choice, or dare,
to find the one with whom to share,
a life of love, a loaf of prayer.

DREAM SEQUENCE II

Scarlet poppies in her hand
are thrown to players
in the all-night band.
Each one plucked one
from the air,
and with a flourish
tucked in hair.
Each one sprouted
with a leaf
which twined around
the loudest notes,
squeezing them
to pulp and juice.
The player's tempo
now came loose,
and, rowdy as a romp in spring
the band gave up its offering.
Then dancing homeward
in a line,
I woke to end my dream sublime.

Stirring now to morning air
I find a scarlet petal
on my side chair.

EXPRESS TRAIN

It does not stop
for me to see more clearly.
The blur of trees
makes one long screen
of privacy.
But, up ahead,
a break, a shard
of light sliced through
those trees
commands my eye.
What do I spy?
An ancient town,
its features spread
in stone and slate,
no wall or garden gate.
It piques my curiosity.
But there's a window
holding me–
in a speeding train
that will not wait.

GEORGIA O'KEEFFE

The desert sands
burn, cry crimson
from an angry sun,
warn me
not to walk here
where she sits,
glowing in the dusk.

The great brush
busy at its work,
raises the rose
to pure applause,
and studs a skull
with it–
life against the
bones of death,
fragrance in the air.

She threads the colors
through her eye,
fashions them to canvas,
sure of where
those ancient hills
trail their purple into blue,
sure of where
the canyons split,
and morning rises, new.

GLOUCESTER

I live close to shore,
close by the men
who go to sea,
who weather sun and storm
alike–they say they are free.
But are they free?
Or only slaves of water,
that vast expanse
which calls them every day.
They cannot stay away,
but must set out
to ply their trade,
to bring their living
to the shore.
They can do no more.
Their fathers did it,
so must they
live to obey the water.
I live close–close enough
to watch them though.

My danger lies on land.

LEGACY II

She makes a point of telling me
the roses came with all this land,
tended well, for fifty years
by grandmother's hand.

And I intend to keep them living
just as long as she
who worked and walked un-tired
among her roses and the bee.

As she walked among her roses
so she walked among her friends,
cultivating through the years
fragrances to live by,
fragrances that never end.

MANHATTAN CITYSCAPE

Each one risen
from the same soil,
they jostle for light,
scaling the wide expanse
of sky.

The old facades
carved in beauty,
stand solid as the brick they wear
–first settlers in this new land–

Now they make room
for steel and glass,
sheets of shimmer
in evening sun.

The stranger still is welcome
and finds the open door,
making his way
among the crowd.
The city streams with light.

And ships are still arriving.
The skyline spreads
its mantle out.
A song of recognition
murmurs on the waters.
For this we came. For this we stay.

MILITARY CEMETERY

Ignoring rain,
we stood alone
among the rows
of names.
All that was left of them
carved in stone.

From ancient scripts
we reconstruct a life–
a body strong and fit,
eager for the living.

But all was left behind
in favor of the dying.
They must have thought
it all worth while.
Then who are we to question?

MUSIC

I hear it without instruments–
that undertone of sand
murmuring on the seaside,
filtering through the land.
I hear it in the rustle
of the swirling autumn leaves
and lilting notes the sparrow trills
never to retrieve.
And in the golden whisper
of gently swaying grain
bits of ancient lullabies
come back to me again.

I do not say an orchestra
is doing any wrong, but
listen all around you
to the syncopated song.
The cricket and the oriole,
the thunder in the storm,
music reigns imperial
from evening until dawn.

ROYALTY II

Light in such a little thing,
enough
to make the angels sing,
and yet he came
in tiny form
like you and me–
carried, then born.
And every year
he comes again
to hearts worn thin
with care and pain.
He hopes to find
a place within.
After all–he is the King.

SHE KNOWS HER STRENGTH

The ancient sea
spat out her rage,
and laughed her spume abroad;
tossed her head
of rumpled curls
against the giant rocks.

Her arrogant roar
engorged the day,
crescendoed to the sky.
Ecstatic
in such bracing air,
she revelled in the play.

With all desire gratified
and energy well spent,
she combed her hair
in gentle waves,
humming a song of wry content.

SUNRISE COME

Silent in the wings of night
await your cue
to splash new splendor
on another day.
In brazen ecstasy
unfurl each hue,
bleed red through
horizontal bars
of gold.
Unfold your splendor
from the secret sphere
and touch the world
awake–
for day will shake
your colored cloak,
leave it muted
to invoke
the hours of work
in broader light.

THE INVITATION

I've planned
a special Christmas tea,
sent out cards–
please RSVP.
But come to find
our world is rude–
no answer means
please exclude.

But on that one
appointed day,
I set the little Christmas treat,
and left the door so any stray
might see the light,
and feel upon their entering
a welcome, warm and bright.

They came–
the ragged child next door,
the mother, bent
from work she could do no more.
Then from the shadows
skulked the cat
who seemed to know
where it was at.
And brought his lady

sleek and fair
through the open door.

When all were there,
they sang my praise
for such an unexpected feast.
And I felt truly warm inside
for such a happy Christmastide.

TO FALL IN LOVE

What's it like to fall in love–
to fall from grace
so far
that every star cries out,
yet know I'm wanted anyway;
to hear The Voice,
and this time not refuse,
but go because He calls,
go because I choose?

It's like a song
without a sting,
like a flower opening;
it's like so many wondrous things,
but none can tell exactly
how I've fallen into grace.
But I will know
when I see His face.

TONGUES OF SPIRIT

How many
must we listen to
before we really hear?

Before we shut
all noise off
and bring the tongues near
enough to understand
the words we shun in fear,
as every complicated day
completes another year.

And still the words
will not be quenched,
nor lose
their potent power,
but flame into
the darkest nights
searing the heart's proud tower.

UNEXPECTED

Uninvited love came in,
pulled me from despair.
When sunk in murk
and breathing only fetid air,
a stranger's hand
reached through the gloom
(the face I could not see)
determined to release
all the old inhibitors
that would not let me be.

A reprimand was no where found,
nor any word of scorn.
He simply took my hand in his
and whispered gently, "come".

UNNUMBERED

Yes, it was the math
she tried so hard to teach,
but my young mind resisted,
staying well beyond her reach.

But she continued doggedly
grappling with my brain,
explaining things another way,
though with little gain.

The numbers tumbled over each,
got jumbled on the page,
yet prodded by a gentle smile,
I tried hard to engage.

Still the math eluded me,
the computation lost,
but, I learned tenacity
that unaware, she taught.

WHEN GABRIEL CAME

Mary wondered, long and deep
at such a visitation.
Surprised and awed together
at the words of salutation
where holiness,
like some sharp sword
thrust itself upon her.

Consider how a life must change
when news of such proportion
is dropped into a day
possessed with its own motion.

If you believe that Gabriel comes
with messages sublime,
your ear must keep
its opening clear–
listening all the time.

WITHIN HER

How much hope
can a mother hold,
though an angel
warn her well?

And how much fear
for the future
with its looming
gates of hell?

But,
all in one small body
the reconciling grows,
as heaven sends the answer,
His flesh in flesh enclosed.

WIVES

I note the women
clustered by the fence.
Each one ready
with her own defense
of this or that,
the arguments
that fill the day.
And who's to say
mid ebb and flow
of house and child,
mid joy and woe
that each imprints
upon the others
the elements of life–
patience and impatience,
the constancy of peace and strife.

YOUR GARDEN

You went away
and missed it all.

I'll tell you now
what I recall:
The rose went climbing
on the fence,
the vine crawled low
without pretense,
and all the zesty marigolds
were flouncing in their frills.
Hollyhocks grew wild again,
leaned against your windowsills.
Your lilac bush draped over ours,
a friendship I encourage,
and all the while
the herbs grew strong,
verbena, mint, and borage.
Along the lower line of hills
solomon seal looked sagely down
on all the little daffodils.
And guarding your own garden, gated, two
clumps of zebra grass created all the garden's
splendor.
So why leave home to simply wander?

NEW COLLECTIONS

AFRICAN WIFE

She watches the child
near the earthen pot
on the fire
that boils the meat.

She watches the bush
for the glistening eye
hid in the silence
that lions keep.

She watches the rock
for the uncoiled snake
that strikes
like a lick of fire.

And watching the blackness
she thinks wild thoughts,
for the man is away
and the sun long gone.

ANGEL WATCH

An angel, any time of day
may have passed you
in array so bright
you took it for the sun.

So common a mistake
to walk in lesser light,
when megawatts bedazzle
blazing life with glory.

And there *are* angels
up and down the land
like fireflies fanned
and burning bright.

Look for them
ere they take flight.

AT THE PARTY

I scarcely met her gaze,
yet, in the coming days
thought I read her well.
The listless eyes
belie the present merriment.

But those whose business
is to read between the lines
find pain and sorrow
bedded under laughter.

And, as parties go,
there always is an after,
when those you meet
come back–impressions
on the mind–
riddles that you play with,
answers that you hope to find.

AUTUMN

I rattle the leaves
along the path.
The sound of death
plays symphony.
The heaps of fallen greenery
call for solemn requiem,
remembered when
our summer walks
were cooled and calmed,
and all the shade a blessing.
I now recall
how each full branch
stretched its arm
in confidence.

They did not die in vain.

AWAKE

Is there nothing in this midnight hour
to stem the flow of random thoughts
that lapping, overlap,
then slow,
and end in deep futility?

The all-consuming day
when structured definitions
occupy the hours,
there is no room
to let that stream come in.

But, as the evening lowers,
it finds its way through crevices,
insisting, still insisting,
that the flow begin again.

All midnight hours conspire
against the place of dream.
Still half awake,
the running thoughts still gather,
form a new-found stream.

BEAUTY

Behind the whitened fence
tulips grow, and daisies too,
each in their own time.
I notice as they reach their prime
how beauty draws me in,
brings me to the place
of looking closely at a face.
It's there I see how sun and rain
excel at bringing forth again
these precious gems of earth:
cups of gold and scarlet,
whitened petals crowned with mirth.

BEFORE

Before the thaw
my heart lay frozen
to its core,
denying any spring.
But it comes in on cue.
Nothing stops the setting sun.
It does its job, and
plunges earth in darkness.
And I in darkness,
and in cold, unwilling
to surrender,
feel a warmth around me,
feel a stir of openness,
like resurrection
from the dead.

BEYOND REASON

No matter that she left
in wintertime,
with ice and snow
to slow her climb
to cruel despair.

No matter that she chose
to go–
expose herself to elements
out there.

No matter that we looked
for her
each day, to make return,
to organize our thinking
and comb our hair.

Some urgency propelled her
into dare.
We knew not why,
but daily wondered
why she was not here–
but there.

BOOKS EQUAL FRIENDS

Books I have chosen,
read and reread,
quaint or profound,
or simple as bread

have often provoked me,
but only to thought.
Gleaning the fragments,
I struggled, then got.

Others convincingly
gave me the thread
to follow the reasoning
of just what was said.

Still, others I've chosen
are lighter by far,
enjoyed for the laughter,
bright as a star.

But book space grows smaller
as friendships expand,
so deciding to clear
I take each in hand,

look at it longingly,
think through the past,
and the choosing of friendship
that I vowed would last.

Decisions are painful
and come with a cost.
Re–shelving my books,
I vowed none would be lost.

BUTTERFLIES– AFTER ROBERT FROST

Cocoons are lovely,
dark and deep,
where we can safely
have our sleep,
await the promises
we keep
when every garden's ours
for sipping treasures
of the flowers.
Traveling on
we take our fill.
With miles to go
we're seldom still.

GERANIUMS

All summer long
they smiled at me,
each in their own color.
And every bee
delayed its flight
to take its daily succor,
glancing at me
as I sat on the porch
watching with intensity.
I could not help
but be impressed
by this small creature's industry.
It never stopped
to gaze at clouds
or sit around and think,
but kept on sipping into cups
that held its treasured drink.

But now they've flown
with summer days
as autumn hold its torch aloft.
The chairs are stored, and
overnight, the wind comes up,
leaving me with lonely
colored petals on my porch.

HERON

Where does the great
blue heron sleep?
The bird must own
a resting place
among the rustling reeds
where only the moon's
bright vigil, and
the water's lyrical lap
lull her into dreams of joy–
tomorrow's bountiful catch.

JANUARY THOUGHTS

The hardest ground
will have to yield
for spring
to sow its seed.

Embedded ice,
now master,
the sun will strike
and thus concede
that earth
will keep old promises:
the rhubarb,
and the daisy field.

The hardest ground
will have to yield.

POEMS OF EXILE
WHERE IT ALL BEGAN

ADAM AND EVE

Naked and innocent compulsion,
rotting as we revelled
in the seeds of destruction;
sprouted a shame
that defaced our connection,
and maimed the fig that wrapped us
in a bright new seduction.

CONSEQUENCE

There was divine prediction.
And there was an even choice.
But in descending order
they listened to the lesser voice.

Then the terrible swing
of the garden gate
unforseen–
now, too late–
dismissing them to wander free
to face a world that would not be–
but for them.

ADVERSARY

Deceit comes crawling,
as it will.
No need to meet the eye
that sees
beyond the consequence,
beyond the rim
where knowledge
builds a sturdy bridge,
and those are wise
who walk it.

WOMAN

Creation's crown
fashioned in flesh,
pure and jewelled as he.
O what a wonderful crown
for such a king as he!

CHOICE

In the garden
choice was ours.
We chose weeds
instead of flowers,
thorns
instead of crowns.

EDEN

Naked, we approached the tree
and plucked,
and felt the painful ecstasy
of opened eyes and liberty.
Beyond the gate
a widened world unleashed itself,
and we embraced it all:
endless hate,
creation torn,
and death pangs newly born.

IN THE BEGINNING

Just to know
the start of things,
the charge that set
the whole thing off,
willing into form
a pattern to be followed
all the way to death.

Had they known
what they were doing?

The lesser voice
breathed out desire,
and rebel acts
now carried on the wind.
when all they did
was heed the rasp,
the curling tongue of lies.

The Greater Voice
now scorned and stilled
made exiles of the two.
And there, outside the garden,
they live the ache of longing,
always longing
for what once they knew.

INHERITANCE

The swing of the eternal gate
began with Adam's exit.
And we like sheep
follow him
in perfect disobedience.

And wanting clothes,
our nakedness
glares only for the moment,
when He calls
"where are you now?"

And wanting out,
the gate is our deliverance.
The garden of the roses
fades away,
its fragrance lost.
We choose the way of toil and death.
We choose the way of dust.

OH ADAM, WHAT HAVE YOU DONE?
2 Esdras 46:118

Such a question calls to mind
all our past transgression.
The heart is stabbed with guilt.
The mind is scattered here and there,
gathering up the myriad sins
that lie ignored, abandoned.
We play at life, and
scorn Your admonitions,
make excuses to Your face,
and pray Your burning eyes
do not go deeply down
to where the cesspool is,
where Adam's voice
can still be heard.

ONE COUPLE–TWO LEAVES

A leaf was scarcely big enough
to cover all the shame
that dropped itself upon them
when God called out their names.
They failed to see how this one act
broke the back of innocence.
How we who follow in their path
with very little reticence
have stepped outside the garden gate,
its flaming sword still burning,
angel-guarded by the Lord.

OUTSIDE

One day, one act,
the blot upon obedience
broke the back of innocence.

Then shame, then blame,
one cover for their nakedness
–lost souls with no redress.

They left us an inheritance
(collusion is a human dance)
and here, outside the garden
that dance does not abate,
nor does the sword its burning
since the closing of the gate.

SOURCE

From Holy hands
the human seed
was strewn abroad,
and formed our race
in innocence.

But, wasted
on a paltry lie,
that glory did not keep.

From Holy hands
the great expulsion
did its work.

From Holy hands
the pair conceived,
but in corruption
passed the aberrant seed
to generations yet unborn.
Leaving us the consequence–
a fatal world in which to breed.

THE EVIL ONE

Determined
as you always are
to twist the truth,
you lie in wait
for righteousness
to speak its mind,
then take the shine
and tarnish it;
change it
from a band of gold
to brass–
unrecognizable.
A chemistry of evil
filtered through each day.

THE TWO OF US

Somewhere in Eden
we lost our way.
Unsatisfied with
what was there,
we shunned the Voice,
embraced the disobedience
that slyly turned our heads.
So it only took a whisper
to fill us with ourselves.
And trapped inside this arrogance
that will not let us go,
we live our lives as fugitives
and strangers in an alien land.

AFTER WORDS

The fruit hung–
and for the pair
the Voice of warning stung.
Then slithering forth
the serpent spoke
with arrogant flair,
countering the Maker
of his tongue;
beguiling the couple
where they stood
pondering a life–
Could it be that good?

Exiting the garden gate
they realized all too late
this paradise was no more home.
Vagabonds, destined to roam,
fearing the night,
cursing the day
when brazenly they dared
disobey.

TWENTIETH CENTURY ADAM AND EVE

As aliens yearn
for the native land,
we still return
to the garden–
taste ancient fruit,
graft seasoned sins
onto new generations.

AFTER ADAM

Sometimes, we remember
to peek through the garden gate,
relive our days of wonder,
our nights of starlit praise.

Sometimes, we recall the One
who made us as we are,
but we disdained the promise,
then the gate was left ajar.
Left for us to wander
in this world of tangled tales
we tell ourselves to fool ourselves
when the siren voice prevails.

Sometimes, only sometimes
when we listen, we can hear
the whispers in the garden
through the stillness–
It is hard to bear.

www.ingramcontent.com/pod-product-compliance
Ingram Content Group UK Ltd.
Pitfield, Milton Keynes, MK11 3LW, UK
UKHW041411180426
11947UKWH00007B/71